# The Best Nest

By Cameron Macintosh

Whip sat on his nest and looked up at Flip and Brill.

"My nest is the best!" he yelled at them.

"I am happy with this nest," said Flip.

"Whip is a pest!" said Brill.

"That nest is **not** good,"
yelled Whip.
"And you can not sit
in my nest."

"I must get some buds
for this nest," said Whip.

But when he was away,
a big gust came.

It hit the nests!

Whip's nest fell!

It fell in the dust.

"I lost my nest!" said Whip.

"We can lift your nest up, Whip," said Flip.

Flip, Brill and Whip got the nest back up.

"You are the best pals,"
said Whip.
"Your nest **is** the best!"

# CHECKING FOR MEANING

1. What did Whip yell at Flip and Brill? *(Literal)*

2. How did Whip's nest fall out of the tree? *(Literal)*

3. Why did Whip say Flip and Brill had the best nest? *(Inferential)*

# EXTENDING VOCABULARY

| | |
|---|---|
| **pest** | What is a *pest*? Why did Brill say that Whip was a pest? |
| **gust** | What is a *gust* of wind? Does a gust come suddenly or slowly? |
| **dust** | What is *dust*? What causes the ground to be dusty? |

# MOVING BEYOND THE TEXT

1.  Have you ever held a bird's nest? What did it feel like? What type of bird did it belong to?

2.  What do birds use to build their nests? Where do they get these things from?

3.  Talk about the size of birds' nests. How big are they? Are they all the same? Why?

4.  Do all birds build their nests in a tree? Where else can they be?

# SPEED SOUNDS

| ft | mp | nd | nk | st |
|----|----|----|----|----|

# PRACTICE WORDS

best

nest

pest

must

gust

nests

dust

lost

lift

and